FAMILY

REUNION

Books by Paul Zimmer

The Ribs of Death
The Republic of Many Voices
The Zimmer Poems
With Wanda: Town and Country Poems
The Ancient Wars

Selected & New Poems

FAMILY REUNION

PAUL ZIMMER

University of Pittsburgh Press

Published by the University of Pittsburgh Press, Pittsburgh, Pa. 15260
Feffer and Simons, Inc., London
Manufactured in the United States of America

Library of Congress Cataloging in Publication Data

Zimmer, Paul.
  Family reunion.

  (Pitt poetry series)
  I. Title. II. Series.
  PS3576.I47F3 1983   811'.54   82-23719
  ISBN 0-8229-3480-9
  ISBN 0-8229-5352-8 (pbk.)

Certain of these poems have appeared in the following magazines, some in slightly altered forms. The author and publisher wish to express their grateful acknowledgments to: *Black Warrior Review, Chariton Review, Chowder Review, Counter/Measures Magazine, Crazy Horse, Field, Hearse, Heatherstone Press Garland Volume, New Letters, Pearl, Poetry Northwest, Poetry Now, Porch, Quarterly West, Rapport,* and *Salmagundi.*

"Barney Hung Over" is reprinted from *Cedar Rock.* "The History of Bears" originally appeared in *The Missouri Review.* "Zimmer with Lester Under the Moon" first appeared in *The North American Review,* copyright © 1973 by the University of Northern Iowa. "Death Demonstrates His Presence to Zimmer" was first published in *Northwest Review.* "Rollo's Miracle," "Zimmer Directs Himself Home from the Diggings," and "Zimmer Fearing Anemia" are reprinted from *The Ohio Review.* "A Zimmershire Lad" first appeared in *Prairie Schooner.* "Father Animus and Zimmer" was originally published in *Three Rivers Poetry Journal.* "What Zimmer Would Be" and "Christiaan Fearing the Sky" are reprinted with permission from the April, 1972 and February, 1976 issues, respectively, of *Yankee Magazine,* published by Yankee, Inc., Dublin, N. H.

The author also wishes to thank Slow Loris Press, Dryad Press, and October House, Inc., for permission to reprint poems from his previous books: *The Ancient Wars; The Zimmer Poems* and *With Wanda: Town and Country Poems;* and *The Republic of Many Voices.*

*The publication of this book is supported by grants
from the National Endowment for the Arts
in Washington, D.C., a Federal agency,
and the Pennsylvania Council on the Arts.*

with love
to Suzanne, Erik, and Justine

Here the trees, timber or fruit-bearing as the case may be, make the wayside hedges ragged by their drip and shade, their lower limbs stretching in level repose over the road, as though reclining on the insubstantial air. At one place, on the skirts of Blackmoor Vale, where the bold brow of High-Stoy Hill is seen two or three miles ahead, the leaves lie so thick in autumn as to completely bury the track. The spot is lonely, and when the days are darkening the many gay charioteers now perished who have rolled along the way, the blistered soles that have trodden it, and the tears that have wetted it, return upon the mind of the loiterer.

—*Thomas Hardy,*
The Woodlanders

CONTENTS

CONTENTS

CONTENTS

I

ZIMMER AT THE DIGGINGS

It is best to begin in the morning with
Low sun slanting over the cool site.
I brush dust from grooves of
Ancient trash, strip down layers,
Sift, count, dig, date the axeheads.

These are my findings:
Surface—Bones of wild dogs,
Some elm stumps, smelling of urine.
Second level—Residue of hemp,
Circular mounds of earth, post holes
Testing of blood, scattered bones of
Children, birds, woodchucks, snakes,
The femur of a stupendous cave bear.
Third level—Reasons for the circles,
A ring of inscribed sandstone tablets sunk
Into mounds of cranial fragments, eye teeth,
Delicate shard and fingerbones.

By midafternoon I begin to sweat under
High sun, the sky presses down on my head,
The axeheads flutter like broken wings.
I begin to glue the shard together,
Rack the teeth, stack the bones
And string them with muscle and sinew.
I breathe on them and listen for voices.

At last, in heat, I wander into the countryside,
Gathering the small, exquisite things I love;
Maple seeds, phlox petals, flakes of birch bark,
Gypsum pebbles, baby mice, all minute jewels.

In my great warmth and confusion
I put them into my mouth and chew them,
Let my teeth commit their quick atrocities.
Then in highest hopes I swallow them,
Feel their pulp and grit slide delicately
Down my throat into the dark acids.

I return to the shade of the site,
Small beauty pumping out to the edges
Of my body, infusing into my parts.
Amidst the circle of tremendous stones
I feel my cells divide in fragile ecstasy.

ZIMMER IN GRADE SCHOOL

In grade school I wondered
Why I had been born
To wrestle in the ashy puddles,
With my square nose
Streaming mucus and blood,
My knuckles puffed from combat
And the old nun's ruler.
I feared everything: God,
Learning and my schoolmates.
I could not count, spell or read.
My report card proclaimed
These scarlet failures.
My parents wrung their loving hands.
My guardian angel wept constantly.

But I could never hide anything.
If I peed my pants in class
The puddle was always quickly evident,
My worst mistakes were at
The blackboard for Jesus and all
The saints to see.
                    Even now
When I hide behind elaborate masks
It is always known that I am Zimmer,
The one who does the messy papers
And fractures all his crayons,
Who spits upon the radiators
And sits all day in shame
Outside the office of the principal.

ZIMMER'S HEAD THUDDING
AGAINST THE BLACKBOARD

At the blackboard I had missed
Five number problems in a row,
And was about to foul a sixth,
When the old, exasperated nun
Began to pound my head against
My six mistakes. When I cried,
She threw me back into my seat,
Where I hid my head and swore
That very day I'd be a poet,
And curse her yellow teeth with this.

ONCE AS A CHILD I HAD BAD DREAMS

Lightning ignited the treetops,
Funnels dropped like fast freights,
One writhed and struck at me.
I looked up its eye to the fires
Of hell and woke screaming.
There was my mother holding me.
A steam tent hissed in my room.
A faint light. I was very warm.
She sang a French song for me,
Stroked my brow with love,
Gave me the comfort of woman.

Now I will make this poem with the wish
That it might assume her fear,
That it would sing the storms away
From her, that it could die for her,
Who has become her own suffering.
I wish this poem could be her pain
So she could walk away from it,
Returning to dignity and sureness.
I would have it fill the lonely void
She told me women always feel
Beyond the comprehension of all men.

for my mother

ZIMMER GUILTY OF THE BURNT GIRL

Once a week
The burnt girl came peddling to our house,
Touching her sweet rolls with raisin fingers,
Her raw face struggling like a bubble
Through lava to say what she had
To sell and why, "Please buy my sweets
To mend my face."

Always I hid behind the piano and heard
My unflinching mother quietly buy a few,
And imagined apricots shriveling in sun,
Spiders boiling and dripping above matches.
Always, when the burnt girl had gone,
I heard my mother drop her purchase
In the rubbish to be burned and
I came out to see the pink graftings,
The horrid, sugared layers of the rolls.

I do not want
The burnt girl to come again.
I am guilty for her and of her.
Always in fever I think of that face.
Sometimes in love I believe that I am
Fire consuming myself, and the burnt girl
Suffers from my love as she sells
Her rolls to mend her face.

IRENE GOGLE

Bugs lived in her hair.
Her one dress was weary.
The nuns were kind
But kept their distance.
When she read aloud
The tedious clock ticked
Between her words.

"Go-go!" we called her.
"Go-go is your girlfriend!"
—when we wished to insult
Another boy. I loathed her
Aloud with the rest;
Once, on a dare, pushed
Her into a classmate so
He could feel her breasts.
The nun broke a yardstick
Over our cowering backs.

On the playground she would
Stand alone by the fence,
Bouncing a dirty tennis ball,
Pretending to be cheerful.

Why should she come to
My mind again? I say words
To my grade-school son:
Kindness, love, compassion.
I pray to God for definitions.

for Erik

ONE FOR THE LADIES AT
THE TROY LAUNDRY WHO COOLED
THEMSELVES FOR ZIMMER

The ladies at the Troy Laundry pressed
And pressed in the warm fog of their labor.
They cooled themselves at the windows,
The steam rising from their gibbous skins
As I dawdled home from school.
In warmer weather they wore no blouses
And if I fought the crumbling coke pile
To the top, they laughed and waved
At me, billowy from their irons.

Oh man, the ladies at the Troy Laundry
Smelled like cod fish out of water
And yet the very fur within their armpits
Made me rise wondering and small.

Zumer Is Icumen In

Zumer is icumen in.
Lewdly sing whohoo;
Floweth hed and gloweth red
And bringth the nuhdie too.
Sing whohoo!
Owlhe bloteth after ram,
Druleth over calfe cu;
Bumper riseth, butte sizeth;
More he sing whohoo.
Whohoo   Whohoo!
Wel sing whohoo nu!
Sing whohoo nu! Sing whohoo!
Sing whohoo nu!

WANDA AND ZIMMER

Wanda, my pussy willow, cupcake,
My chinchilla red rabbit,
I wanted to love you so much,
To chase you into corners and
Pet you till your ears lay down,
Till the membranes drew back
From over your rosy eyes.
I wanted to make you breathe easily,
But you didn't love me,
Ran like hell when you saw me,
Flicked up your fine, hind legs
When I came near and pissed
On my pants legs.
           Wanda, I was
Always afraid to break you
But still you were frightened
Of my fingers, teeth and groin,
Certain that if I held you
Your small bones would bend
And crack off one another,
Your organs crush together
In the agony of my affection.

WHAT ZIMMER WOULD BE

When asked, I used to say,
"I want to be a doctor."
Which is the same thing
As a child saying,
"I want to be a priest,"
Or
"I want to be a magician,"
Which is the laying on
Of hands, the vibrations,
The rabbit in the hat,
Or the body in the cup,
The curing of the sick
And the raising of the dead.

"Fix and fix, you're all better,"
I would say
To the neighborhood wounded
As we fought the world war
Through the vacant lots of Ohio.
"Fix and fix, you're all better,"
And they would rise
To fight again.
                    But then
I saw my aunt die slowly of cancer
And a man struck down by a car.

All along I had really
Wanted to be a poet,
Which is, you see, almost
The same thing as saying,
"I want to be a doctor,"
"I want to be a priest,"
Or
"I want to be a magician."
All along, without realizing it,
I had wanted to be a poet.

FATHER ANIMUS AND ZIMMER

Father Animus asked who broke
The window in the sacristy,
I went head-on into evil,
Lying through my new incisors.

Holy Ghost moaned in my guts.
The light bulbs swayed on
Their cords in the Parish
As each freckle on my face
Became a venial sin.

Father Animus asked his question,
My answer tangled in memories
Of ardor in the cozy parish:

How springtime I would swing up
Into dogwood trees in the churchyard,
Let the dark eyes of the blossoms read
Me like a breviary. Summertime
I ran the baselines as though
They were the shadow of the spire.

In fall, exploring the attic
Of the old grade school,
I became my own history in
The dust, finding my father's
Initials carved in a broken desk,
My aunts' and uncles' first communions
Crumbling in antique records.

One winter, when the janitor
Had sprained his ankle, I climbed
Up inside the steeple to free
The bell rope, rung after rung,
Through drafts and timberings.
Bats retreated, wind screeched
Outside through the slate shingles.

I felt I was rising in the head
Of Father Animus, through warnings
And pronouncements, his strict,
Reluctant love diminishing as
I aspired, choked, deprived
Of space as I climbed higher.

Father Animus asked who
Broke the sacristy window
And the cross on the spire,
Tucking in its legs,
Flew away in sorrow.

THE DAY ZIMMER LOST RELIGION

The first Sunday I missed Mass on purpose
I waited all day for Christ to climb down
Like a wiry flyweight from the cross and
Club me on my irreverent teeth, to wade into
My blasphemous gut and drop me like a
Red hot thurible, the devil roaring in
Reserved seats until he got the hiccups.

It was a long cold way from the old days
When cassocked and surpliced I mumbled Latin
At the old priest and rang his obscure bell.
A long way from the dirty wind that blew
The soot like venial sins across the schoolyard
Where God reigned as a threatening,
One-eyed triangle high in the fleecy sky.

The first Sunday I missed Mass on purpose
I waited all day for Christ to climb down
Like the playground bully, the cuts and mice
Upon his face agleam, and pound me
Till my irreligious tongue hung out.
But of course He never came, knowing that
I was grown up and ready for Him now.

CONFESSION, CURSE AND PRAYER

I confess all creatures I have killed:
Flies, mosquitoes, roaches, ants in number;
Sowbugs, moths, grasshoppers, and bees;
Also beetles, snails, spiders to less degree;
Then two snakes, a quail, four frogs,
One baby robin and a rabbit stoned
In a seizure of youthful cruelty;
Two mangled woodchucks and a dying cat in mercy;
Many fish, some crabs, once a chicken,
Toads, worms and a butterfly or two.
Thus I am steeped in death like any man.

I recall so many of their resignations:
The first shock and brief fluttering,
The eyes turning slowly into themselves,
Or the small shell suddenly crushed
While the limbs still twitch and clutch
At the final glimmers of perception,
At the irretrievable thing that is gone;
And I am guilty of these destructions.

God damn the man who calls this sentimentality!
Who could not think of these things
Without praying for a quiet mind?
Let nothing cruel stir in my blood again.

for Justine

ZIMMER THE DRUGSTORE COWBOY

At least I know my peculiar emptiness,
My vague reality, as though
I'd been stunned by a concrete tit at birth,
Dull as a penny bouncing off a cinder block;
My white socks down over high tops,
The big lugs heavy with gravel and mud.

I always get up in the early morning,
Sit on the drugstore bench in the mist,
Drink Dr. Peppers for breakfast until
The boys at the Shell station start
Revving their motors like a pride of lions.
I wait all day for things to cool down,
Watch the bread trucks and big rigs
Deliver and depart, pass out of my sight
Down the Interstate.
                              I get mad about things:
Shattered safety glass in the streets.
The stupid heat lightning swelling out of trees,
Groove, gash, dent, dog, mosquito, fly;
Once in a while something just froths me,
Anger bursting through my skin and slapping
Surface like the side of a bluegill,
My cold, bony mouth snapping and sucking
At the hot air, my eyeballs pivoting
Until I can settle down again.

At night I walk the town, look up through
The tiny squares of window screens,
Inside the squares of pictures and doorframes,
Inside the glowing squares of television,
Inside the squares of the windows.

Everything is plumb and solid in the night,
The corners of lamplight fastening things down.
Wherever I move the darkness moves
Because I have become my own shadow.
Crickets tinker with the silence.
I walk in the dim alleys, see stars
Well out of the roofs of buildings.
They swarm and multiply like a mass
Of tiny gnats in my gaze. I wonder
How many I could see if I watched forever?
Star growing into star, year after year,
New revelations spreading beyond my sight,
Massing until they would all grow together,
Swelling like heat lightning out of trees.
Then maybe I could live like a bluegill
All of the time, full of hunger and purpose,
Cool, trim, quick in the water,
One little muscle waiting to strike.

II

"What have you been reading?" I asked. "A book," he said. It was on the ground on the other side of him. So I would not have to bother to look over his knees to see it, he said, "A good book."

Then he told me, "In the part I was reading it says the Word was in the beginning, and that's right. I used to think water was first, but if you listen carefully you will hear that the words are underneath the water."

—Norman Maclean,
A River Runs Through It

WANDA BEING BEAUTIFUL

To be beautiful is to somehow keep
A dozen fires burning at night,
To know that all eyes shining
Out of the trees are afraid of you.
It is to know that every crackle of
A twig, every footfall is a threat,
That desire is greatest from a distance.
To be beautiful is to stay on the move
Through every season, to watch sharply
As you take what you want; but mostly
It is knowing how to choose dry wood,
How to bank your fires against cold.

WANDA AND THE FISH

She told him that she could not do this thing;
He heard only the rumbling of heavy currents.
She said she wanted to with all her heart
But could not; that everything she had been told
By God and man made this an evil thing to do;
That she loved him, but could not do this thing.

Harking only to cold blood grinding through his meat,
To what the moon whispered as it pressed upon
His back, he went on against her protests.
When it was over he disappeared into the depths.

Still, after all these years, she dreams of him.
He becomes a fish fanning and holding in currents.
She shows herself and he strikes with all his might,
Sand and bits of weed swirl up around them;
He devours her, makes her one with his flesh,
Carries her forever in the folds of his silver brain.

BARNEY HUNG OVER

Last night I murdered a thousand cells
In my brain with beer. It will be
Months before they renew themselves.
I am in pain and feel cold. I check
My abdomen for long, raw wounds.

We were all riding high for hell,
Slugging down draughts, arm wrestling,
Pinballs flashing under our eyebrows
Scarred as blue as cue chalk.

Then Wanda flounced in, sat down on
A bar stool, ordered a cold glass of wine.
She looked sweet enough to swallow.
We all began flexing, showing our plumage.

Suddenly there were raw steaks
In the air, we were choosing up sides,
Spilling out to the alley for the fight
Like billy goats driving spikes with
Our skulls. Wanda stayed with her drink.

The rest is muddied in my mind,
The thud, scuffle and shock of it,
Someone down on blacktop, kicking out,
Then a thrust and slash, guts spilling
Blind as worms in the air, the spatter
Of surprised blood, limbs slowing down,
Everything growing cold and coldest,
All of us stumbling, running away
Under the moon that lurched through
The trees-of-heaven.
                              And Wanda never
Looked outside to see what happened.

THE EISENHOWER YEARS

Flunked out and laid-off,
Zimmer works for his father
At Zimmer's Shoes for Women.
The feet of old women awaken
From dreams, they groan and rub
Their hacked-up corns together.
At last they stand and walk in agony
Downtown to Zimmer's fitting stool
Where he talks to the feet,
Reassures and fits them with
Blissful ties in medium heels.

Home from work he checks the mail
For greetings from his draft board.
After supper he listens to Brubeck,
Lays out with a tumbler of Thunderbird,
Cigarettes and *From Here to Eternity.*

That evening he goes out to the bars,
Drinks three pitchers of Stroh's,
Ends up in the wee hours leaning
On a lamp post, his tie loosened,
Fedora pushed back on his head,
A Chesterfield stuck to his lips.

All of complacent America
Spreads around him in the night.
Nothing is moving in this void,
Only the feet of old women,
Twitching and shuffling in pain.
Zimmer sighs and takes a drag,
Exhales through his nostrils.
He knows nothing and feels little.
He has never been anywhere
And fears where he is going.

for my father

A Zimmershire Lad

Oh what a lad was Zimmer
  Who would rather swill than think,
Who grew to fat from trimmer,
  While taking ale to drink.

Now his stomach hangs so low,
  And now his belt won't hook,
Now his cheeks go to and fro
  When he leaps across a brook.

Oh lads, ere your flesh decay
  And your sight grows dimmer,
Beware the ale foam in your way
  Or you will end like Zimmer.

THE CURSE OF THE FROGS

Once, in Louisville on pass from basic training,
Zimmer drank so much beer he got hiccoughs.
He swilled on until he could not speak,
Could not remember name, rank or serial number
And staggered from his stool out to the night
To somewhere find a room and fall to bed.

All night his bladder stretched and ached.
He dreamt of those frogs they used to catch
Beside the creek, how Barney would turn them
Over to spread their legs apart and slip
A reed up through the anus, then slowly blow
The creatures up like green balloons,
To bob and turn upon the foam. All night
Zimmer watched them float in agony,
Their small eyes bulging with shock and revenge.
Only their mouths moved slightly.

If he could now, Zimmer would swagger into The Palms
Again to drink Stroh's draught with his buddies,
Sharing all the flat-footed, artless talk,
The smoky drift of their potentiality,
Round after round when anything seemed possible.

But then he remembers the night
Barney and Gus lurched out to the pick-up
And roared off for Wanda's in smoke and cinders,
Forgetting the curve just past the Sohio station.
Gus went through the windshield and broke
Against an elm stump; Barney was crushed
Between the steering post and truck bed.
The very next month Zimmer was drafted.

THE SWEET NIGHT
BLEEDS FROM ZIMMER

Imbellis, the bully, catches me in the dark
With no sunlight I can squirm through.
His body uncoils its frustrations,
Fists plunge like the last stones
Of a landslide.
          Pain flies
To my surfaces as though it had
Always been there waiting for
Imbellis to challenge it out.
My skin folds back in slots and tabs,
The sweet night bleeds from my face.

Imbellis catches me in a dark place,
His jaws and pincers grinding.
I feel my brains sucked out of my head,
My heart clutched in his claws,
Remembering and still trying to beat.
I am ground up and spat into the weeds.
The sweet night is bleeding from my skull.

Imbellis catches me in a dark place
And stars descend to coil about my head,
Buzzing about my gravity, sinking
Their stingers in my lips and eyelids.
In the trees each twig and sucker
Is pointing at a separate fire.
How could I have forgotten all these stars?

*

Stars in the desert faded at dawn;
Then the flash and shock wave rammed
Sand in my face, uprooted cactus,
Blasted the animals, birds from the sky.

29

Afterwards, under the fireball
And faint stars, we wanted to kick
Dead rabbits, throw stones at each other,
Call each other sons-of-bitches.

❀

Once on a lake at night I dropped
My line between stars and prayed
For fish in midst of the universe.
The small pickerel swallowed my hook
And when I ripped it out the fish
Screamed like a wounded rabbit.
I rowed my boat in out of the gloom,
Churning the galaxies and nebulae,
Spoiling the perfect night.

❀

Imbellis caught me in a dark place.
He won't back off and let me be.
I look for a place to hide under
Mother's navel, behind father's penis.
But I can't remember who I am.
Someone wounded and breathing hard,
A sorry man trying to enter the earth.

THE HISTORY OF BEARS

The bear came out of night,
Shambling and humming to itself
Until it smelled man in the cave.
The hair on its back stood up.
It groaned and tossed its head.

Bear looked into the cave and saw
Its images on walls and ceiling,
Saw Zimmer cowering in the corner.
Bear sniffed again and went away.

Zimmer feared the bear like God.
He watched until it gave in
To its years, then cut it open,
Ate the sacred marrow from its bones,
The brain from its ponderous skull,
Trying to learn the love of bear.

*

The bear lopes in the morning,
Its fur pungent and steaming,
Its drool spattering the frost.
Last night the noise of Zimmer's dogs
Ripped through its uneasy sleep.
Today it will retreat once more
Over the crumbled, primal asphalt,
Past the gray, broken shanties
And tangles of old copper wire.

*

The bear smells ancient stories
Under the turf, scattered bones
And teeth of terrible encounters.

31

He rips his claws down the maple bark
And laps at the redolent sap.
He hears how the wind desires
The trees, how storms make them
Bow and dip their canopies in
Strange light; he drinks cold sludge
From the creek and moves on.

❋

Zimmer loves what the bear has lost:
Sun through new leaves and dazzle
Of fish in thrashing currents,
Berries on the logging roads,
Bees nests in broken elms
And long dreams under the snow.

ZIMMER ENVYING ELEPHANTS

I have a wide, friendly face
Like theirs, yet I can't hang
My nose like a fractured arm
Nor flap my dishpan ears.
I can't curl my canine teeth,
Swing my tail like a filthy tassel,
Nor make thunder without lightning.

But I'd like to thud amply around
For a hundred years or more,
Stuffing an occasional tree top
Into my mouth, screwing hugely for
Hours at a time, gaining weight,
And slowly growing a few hairs.

Once in a while I'd charge a power pole
Or smash a wall down just to keep
Everybody loose and at a distance.

THE ANCIENT WARS

Dear Imbellis:

When I think of the old days
I start to bleed again,
Recalling my terrified exits;
The alleys and swamps I hid in;
Your fists exploding in my face
And the light fog of concussions.
I wonder, old bull, old turk,
Old hammer, if we passed
Each other on the street,
Would your anger spill out
Again over your eye rims?
Would your ears redden
Like a rooster's wattle,
Would you knock my bridge
Back down my throat and beat
My glasses back into my dim eyes?
I like to think that
By now you have relented,
That some woman or work
Has doused your fires,
That if we met again we would
Slap each other on the back
And laugh about the ancient wars.
Imbellis, old bravo, super pug,
Could we be friends now?
Would you let me forgive you?

                              Peace,
                              Zimmer

34

Dear Zimmer,

Remember how you loved the Friday Night Fights?
That was always you and me in the ring,
Circling, jabbing, throwing classy combinations
Until the abrupt explosion, my fists crashing
Down like boulders, your body suddenly limp;
You collapsing as a hammered cow into
Your own spit and blood as the crowd
Came to its feet growling and hooting;
You on the canvas flapping and quaking,
You crawling up the ropes to your feet
And me sledging you down again
And you screaming at the television,
"Stop it! Stop it!" Remember?

Zimmer, start sweating again.
I am waiting for you still,
Maybe around the next corner.
One day you'll come
Blundering into my sights again;
When you do I'll clean your clock
But good, shred your cheeks,
Roll your bloody teeth,
Crunch your jewels and punch
Your dim lights out forever.

Yours,
Imbellis

THE DOGS OF ZIMMER

The tether of the aeons holds them.
There is order and habit in their love.
But sometimes they turn on each other
In frustration, snarling and flashing teeth.
On moonlit nights they grow restless,
Hearing things that they cannot see.
They chew on pillows, wet the rugs.

A busy man should have perfect dogs,
But Zimmer's dogs go flick, flick, flick,
Moaning and thumping the floorboards.
They tongue his hand in the night
And make him get up to pee.

Sometimes when he unchains them,
They whisk away before he can call
Them back. He does not know
Where they go or what they do.
He spends hours wistfully calling them,
Imagines how they snuffle post holes,
Raise their dingy hinders to great stones
Or tunnel into ancient graves.

But always when it seems worst,
That they have gone wild into woods,
Joining packs to overrun the suburbs,
It's flick, flick, flick outside his windows,
And Zimmer opens to see them smiling.
The wild lights in their eyes grown dim,
They bang the doorway with their tails.

CHRISTIAAN FEARING THE SKY

When I think that Wanda doesn't love me
I begin to dream about ways
I might die, swearing to myself
That my death will not be humble.
The bad dreams clutch into my sleep
And snap like lowbound lightning.
All possibilities are massive
And spectacular: I am struck in
A vacant lot by meteorites, split by
Foreign matter from scalp to testicles.

Or I blow suddenly apart like a supernova,
Rotate, burn, fuse and fly asunder in
Six directions, arms flying east and west,
Stomach north, buttocks south, feet driving
Deep into the earth, while my head
Rises and spreads in the stratosphere,
Glowing purple and capped with ice.

But always, despite despair I am renewed,
Knowing that my matter cannot be destroyed.
The memory of Wanda restores itself in
Emptiness like a small, sticky bird pecks
Out of its egg or an insect grows larger
Than itself and splits its husk.
My cells go on secretly dividing.
The stack of my backbones braces and holds.

I GO OUT IN THE LONG NIGHTS

Dear Wanda,

I go out in the long nights to
Stars again, measure and track
The dazzle, sense numbers meshing
Like gears in the ancient voids.
I feel my excited body try to shine
Out to those farflung corners.

I always look for you in the lens,
See galaxies coiling and spreading,
The flexing of the nebulae,
Startled vacuums of the black holes.
Scanning the horizons, I pretend
That you are the great star blinking
On the north rim, though I know
It is only Arcturus descending.

I swear mine is the only warmth in
The universe, the one intelligent sign.
The rest is only frigid silence.

But Wanda, when I seek you in
The stars, I remember all our warm,
Deliberate movements on the tracks
Of the great night. I still wonder
Where you might be in all this glister.

Love,
Christiaan

JULIAN BARELY MISSES
ZIMMER'S BRAINS

The end of winter seeped up
Through our boots.
                    Julian and I
Were hunting over the fields
For things that splayed
The deep, confident tracks in
The final snow, when Julian
Slipped on a viscid clod
And his shotgun cracked
Both barrels past my ear.

My God, my God, I see it yet!

I sit down on a cold stone
And feel my chubby brains
Float down like stuffing from
Old cushions, I feel my face
Rammed back through the grinder
Of my teeth and birds
Returning to fork me apart
Like tender meat.

Yet I am alive to tell you that
Ducks applauded overhead and game
Flicked all about, but Julian
And I had enough of shooting.

Now the only heavy footprints in
The snow are ours.
                    Spring
Has come and I am alive
With the sense that I am still alive.

CECIL, ZIMMER, AND
THE MAN-MADE LAKE

The dam was built in
A month and the river
Mixed with the creeks
And accrued.
        "Big fish!"
Cecil said, oiling our reels,
Checking our lines. In a week
A shallow lake had formed;
Ten days more it rose above
The tree tops in the valley.

"Just like filling the tub,"
Cecil said, "Try flies first, Zimmer,
Then spinners, spoons and plugs."
We tried them all. No good.
Then baited our hooks with worms,
Shiners, frogs and salmon eggs,
Until the lake rose up to
The level of our aspirations.

"Tomorrow we troll," Cecil said,
"Then gig, jig, use electric rods!"
But next day the lake had filled
Our basement with excrement,
Old tires and rusty cans; the kitchen
Filled, then the living room.
It rose to the second floor and
Flooded our beds.
              "Kill the bastards
With your hands!" said Cecil.
"Grab them by the gills and
Beat their goddamned scales off!"
But we had time only to swim
Up the chimney and paddle
Like hell for shore.

40

Leaves of Zimmer

You Zimmer! Whimpering, heavy, mumbling, lewd;
Does America sing you a sad song?
It is a trifle! Resign yourself!
Nothing is without flaw.
Confess that you feel small buds unclutching again!
Confess that the rich sod turns up to you always
*   as your lover!*
By God! Accept nothing less than this for
*   affection:*
The stars dangling like green apples on the
*   distant peaks;*
The sea foam combing itself through rocks;
No foofoo can strip you of this!
No mountebanks can take this away!
If one is deprived then all are deprived;
America will love us all or it will not love.
Camerado! Give me your hand.
All of us will go! Boatmen and trappers,
Bridegroom and bride, sailors and drifters,
Woodsmen, mechanics, preachers, lawyers, fishermen,
We must also raise the insulted and injured.
Even the President will come!
If one of us falls the others must wait;
For lacking one, we lack all.
Camerado! My left hand hooks you round the waist,
My right hand points to America.
Let us feel the country under our boot soles;
Let us seek it in the air we breathe.

41

WORRYING ABOUT YOU ALL THE TIME

Dear Wanda,

Worrying about you all the time,
I could just as well be drowning.
I went to see your act last night,
Sat down on my piles, in the doldrums,
My soft teeth aching in the grind,
Eyeballs burning through bifocals.
Then you floated into the spotlight,
Hands, unfolding, folding like sting rays.
The cymbal started to sizzle as
You slipped out of clothes and floated
Them to sharks in the audience.
The circles of your thighs, calves,
Bob and weave of belly, breasts,
Making the whole room sigh and sweat.

And you would give these things away
So easily! The secrets all of us
Had burned to see, you revealed as
Lightly as a perch can lay its eggs.
Even the band saw everything!

Wanda, I went out into the night,
My eyeballs rolled through ashes,
Cold air fired my teeth up,
My hemorrhoids bled with the knowledge
That you aren't precious anymore.

                                    So long,
                                    Cecil

CECIL SLIDING AWAY FROM
THE MEMORY OF WANDA

Wanda is gone and I sweat like concrete
under the bridge; my many shirts
are soaked in their annual rings.
I try to sleep beneath traffic.
All day brown dirt rolls in from
the road and ancient fulcrums groan.
The bridge is between the sky and me,
a full moon rises through its span.
All that I own is under this bridge:
pale weeds, shale, bits of broken glass,
a fractured chair, arches and cantilevers
growing dim like memories of Wanda.
The great brown river slops on past,
my right foot sleeps in its current,
my left shoe is sucked into mud.

There is only one knowledge, one remembrance:
It is rain touching everything at once.
First a faint groaning inward, sagging of air,
then the small whips charge and flatten
across the hollow trunks of thunder,
the lightning firing branch through branch.
Even under the bridge my fingers extend
in rain, trees lean and clods dissolve,
weeds hang on, mosses fuse, all things bend
to the sound of rain and sink toward the river.

And so I feel the claims of the water,
watching everything pass in the river:
car, potty, son, dog, cat, fence, house,
the bloated body of a beautiful woman.
I put both feet in the current, slip into
the brown water, wait for passage also.

In the river I am soft, my body is
eel grass pointing to vague places;
all I can see are the whites of my eyes.
I turn and turn my own circles,
fearing heavy objects, the suddenly
violent rocks and planks, slap and
tangle of shoreline branches. My lungs
burn away with recollections in water.

And I recall first of all festivals:
How I lost my hat in the celebrations,
dancing in the milky stubs of harvest
with Wanda: we flowed in jubilation,
shouted and struck our sticks together,
repeated the names of our pride
and rejoiced in where we had been.

I remember walks in the woods with Wanda
under great weeping elms and chestnuts.
Surprised by brown nuts in their pods,
we ran our thumbs into the damp cushions
where they had grown, felt the knowledge
of the tree, how it remembered and provided
for the long drop from the branches.

Now cell by cell comes winter.
Ripeness collapses in needles of frost,
birds have left their voids like Wanda,
leaves make final decisions,
curl in about the fruit then drop.
Everything bends to this cold water,
the bridge is bobbing in the distance.
I rise and fall with bitter debris.

ENTERING THE STORM, UNABLE TO SWIM, ZIMMER, ROLLO, AND CECIL ARE SAVED

The storm mixed and fell upon the lake,
And chins first, we rammed its wall.
While one man bailed out water and another
Worked the motor, I held the lantern high
And howled for the pinewood shore.
Only the fish we had caught could swim,
And they revived in the slosh of our hull.

The storm hooked my cheeks and beat
My voice back. It swallowed up my light.
It rose faster than our buckets and washed
Our motor out. Our fish began to swim,
And we began to sink. We despaired,
We cursed fish, water, storm, and world.
We defied nine planets and the cosmos.

Then a great voice said, "Rub-a-dub-dub!"
Behold, our boat rose, water drained out,
And the storm uncapped and split above
Our heads! Our fish suffered in the hull again.
And we sailed off believing, believing.

Rollo says, "I can bring down rain."
We say, "Bull crap!" and slug him
On his bicep. But he says,
"Underwear ain't fit to wear!"
And lightning cracks it knuckles,
Thunder pulls the plug out.
Fish could swim in what comes down.

When it lets up we say to Rollo,
"Bull crap, buddy, you got lucky!"
But Wanda is giving Rollo the eye.

"Underwear ain't fit to wear!"
He chants again and the clouds
Uncork, the river starts to rise.
Wanda takes Rollo by the arm,
They go off to meet the rainbow.

We stand there with the cold rain
Sighing in our socks. Cecil says,
"Underwear ain't fit to wear."
"Underwear ain't fit to wear!"
Shouts Zimmer. Lester whispers,
"Underwear ain't fit to wear."
But that sun shines on and on—
Bright as a fresh dropped egg.

LESTER TELLS OF WANDA AND THE BIG SNOW

Some years back I worked a strip mine
Out near Tylersburg. One day it starts
To snow and by two we got three feet.
I says to the foreman, "I'm going home."
He says, "Ain't you staying till five?"
I says, "I got to see to my cows,"
Not telling how Wanda was there at the house.
By the time I make it home at four
Another foot is down and it don't quit
Until it lays another. Wanda and me
For three whole days seen no one else.
We tunneled the drifts, we slid
Right over the barbed wire and laughed
At how our heartbeats melted the snow.
After a time the food was gone and I thought
I would butcher a cow, but then it cleared
And the moon come up as sweet as an apple.
Next morning the ploughs got through. It made us sad.
It don't snow like that no more. Too bad.

LESTER TELLS OF THE END OF SUMMER

Wanda was having an ugly night,
All drawed and pale in her glow,
Rolling her tired bones in the stars,
Through branches of the trees.
We'd drunk wine all day together
And Wanda was worse for wear.
Pock marks yawed in her cheeks,
Her temples pulled in for dryness.
I was the elm that propped her up
But rotted with the blight myself.
Deep in my trunk I felt the sadness.
My leaves knowed things they couldn't tell,
Yearning to fall and loosen in
Slime and dirt, far below moonshine
Down in dark where the old people lay.

ZIMMER WITH LESTER
UNDER THE MOON

Lester thrashes in his blankets,
High bones grinding on low ones,
His teeth rasp like forewings
Of crickets.
        In his sleep
He tells me of his fear:
He thinks Wanda is the moon
That sends the high wind down,
Sniffs at the cracks
Between clapboards and peels
The shingles off.
        I cannot sleep
Near his somnolent terror.
I step out into the frigid wind
And let it suck my breath.

There are no clouds.
But as I watch stars divide
And multiply, the moon arcs high
In the night. It is so full
I could pluck and eat it.
Its light powders the fine bones
Of pine trees and rabbits.
Things expand in its presence.

Lester cannot love this strength
And splendor; he prays for eclipses
Or cloudy nights. I am afraid for him.

Wanda, I don't want to worry anymore.
I want to lie down cold in
My own skin like a snake and
Never be afraid for anyone again.

49

THURMAN DREAMING IN RIGHT FIELD

In right field I am so far out
The batter has unwound before
I hear the crack of his effort,
And the ball whirrs out and bounces
Like the wind off the wall
At idiot angles.
              I am lonely
In that distance.
                The moon shines
Like a long fly in right field
Where the rain falls first
And the snow drifts in the winter.
The sun cuts intricate shadows
From the decks above my head,
And balls, dropping like duck hawks,
Suddenly grow dull in the broken light
Of right field.
             But there is
Always time for dreaming before
The impossible catch, the wheel
And shotgun throw on one bounce to
The plate, where the catcher slams
The ball onto the sliding runner's thigh,
And the crowd goes roaring, "Thurman!"
In that far field where
I am dreaming once again.

THURMAN'S SLUMPING BLUES

One day out in right field
The ball went by me quicker
Than a flushed-out quail.
I wagged my glove at it
But what I got was wind.
Then I fell down like a fool.
Fans stung me harder than
A swarm of bald-faced hornets.
That was what started
The whole damned thing.

I felt the sap run out of my knees,
Looked at my hands, they smelled of fish.
Wanda was up there in the box seats,
Sitting on a whole school of mackerel!

We dropped in the standings.
Pitchers pulled the string
And tied me up in knots.
I went left when I should have gone right.
Wanda commenced to act skittish.
Today I woke up and she was gone.
Over my steak and eggs
The paper tells me that
This is last place.

THE GAMES IN THE FIELD

It took us two days in heat to mow
The field in preparation for the games.
When the bounds were set at last,
Wanda stood solemnly with squirrels
And deer to watch us from the trees.
Lester plunged in the circles and squares,
Julian dashed, Cecil dove at the ball,
Zimmer shouted his taunts and threats
As we tore and strained against each
Other to show our broken, bloody plumage.

Like always, when it was over,
And the results were duly recorded,
Wanda ambled away from us all,
Not caring for our achievements
And keeping her choice to herself.

ZIMMER DRUNK AND ALONE,
DREAMING OF OLD FOOTBALL GAMES

I threw the inside of my gizzard out, splashing
Down the steps of that dark football stadium
Where I had gone to celebrate the ancient games.
But I had been gut-blocked and cut down by
A two-ton guard in one quarter of my fifth.
Fireflies broke and smeared before my eyes,
And the half-moon spiraled on my corneas.
Between spasms the crickets beat halftime to
My tympanum, and stars twirled like fire batons
Inside the darkness. The small roll at my gut's end,
Rising like a cheer, curled up intestine to the stomach,
Quaking to my gullet, and out my tongue again.
Out came old victories, defeats and scoreless ties,
Out came all the quarters of my fifth,
Until exhausted, my wind gone and my teeth sour,
I climbed the high fence out of that dark stadium,
Still smarting from the booing and hard scrimmage.
I zigzagged down the street, stiff-arming buildings,
And giving flashy hip fakes to the lamp posts.
I cut for home, a veteran broken field drunkard,
With my bottle tucked up high away from fumbles.

GUS IN THE STREETS

On hot nights the whole city
Shares industry, the air tastes
Of tarnished coins, cinders sparkle
Through the lamplight and settle
In the cups of my molars.
Even the television grits behind
My eyes, so I walk out into
The smutty streets past alleys
Of old bones and glass, past
The marquees of skin shows
Into the neighborhood of rooms.
Here, where air bites hardest
Into my flesh, I imagine that
Wanda calls me from a doorway,
Her eyes smoldering with consent.

Later, upstairs with an old whore
And tasting ashes again, I wonder
Why Wanda never kept promises.
Why her face, so full of cozy signals,
Had never really intended all
The things I thought it meant.

GUS SEES WANDA DRINKING

When she was drunk
The veins pumped up
In her forehead,
Full lips slathered
The foam of wine.
Once, in her anger,
She spit into my face,
But I did not flinch
Nor wipe it away.
Her fingers grew bony
And red, scrabbling
Like crabs on the bottle.

Once I found her
Weeping in the street
At dawn. When I tried
To help her she
Broke her glass
And threatened to lay
My damp cheeks open.

Nothing had gone right.
She was easy and cheap,
Her perfume was violent,
Her make-up eroded
With sweat and tears
And she was certain
She would die unloved.

To be a woman was hell.
Would I *please* give her
Some change and go away?
She would come home soon.
The sun was coming up.
She needed to rest.
If I gave her money
She would not drink anymore.
She would buy coffee,
Wash her face and never
Frighten me again.

ZIMMER'S LAST GIG

Listening to hard bop,
I stayed up all night
Just like good times.
I broke the old waxes
After I'd played them:
Out of Nowhere, Mohawk,
Star Eyes, Salt Peanuts,
Confirmation, one-by-one;
Bird, Monk, Bud, Fats, Pres,
All dead, all dead anyway,
As clay around my feet.

Years ago I wanted to
Take Wanda to Birdland,
Certain that the music
Would make her desire me,
That after a few sets
She would give in to
Rhythm and sophistication.
Then we could slip off
Into the wee hours with
Gin, chase, and maryjane,
Check into a downtown pad,
Do some fancy jitterbugging
Between the lilywhites.

But Wanda was no quail.
Bud could have passed
Out over the keys,
Bird could have shot
Up right on stage,

Wanda would have missed
The legends. The band
Could have riffed
All night right by
Her ear, she never
Would have bounced.

THE DUKE ELLINGTON DREAM

Of course Zimmer was late for the gig.
Duke was pissed and growling at the piano,
But Jeep, Brute, Rex, Cat and Cootie
All moved down on the chairs
As Zimmer walked in with his tenor.
Everyone knew that the boss had arrived.

Duke slammed out the downbeat for Caravan
And Zimmer stood up to take his solo.
The whole joint suddenly started jiving,
Chicks came up to the bandstand
To hang their lovelies over the rail.
Duke was sweating but wouldn't smile
Through chorus after chorus after chorus.

It was the same with Satin Doll,
Do Nothing Till You Hear From Me,
Warm Valley, In A Sentimental Mood;
Zimmer blew them so they would stay played.

After the final set he packed
His horn and was heading out
When Duke came up and collared him.
"Zimmer," he said, "You most astonishing ofay!
You have shat upon my charts,
But I love you madly."

ZIMMER REMEMBERING WANDA

In my imaginings I wish to drop
Through the long hole into the layers
Of the great mound, pass through
The meanings of ancient cities
Into the fiery lava of earth's core.

Then I see the hole, in my confusion,
The deep remoteness of my dreams
Surrounded by warm, rising limestone,
Dripping with calcium and honey.
I carve its image into stalagmites
And old bones, draw it wide and open
On the walls, spread for fornication,
Mutilation, death by finger, arrow, penis.
I listen for the sigh of its release.

But Wanda rolls away in her emptiness,
Cries me the long sorrow of the hole,
Tells me all the fathoms of her loneliness,
How only the sea can be her lover.

Then I see Wanda of the warm salt rind,
Her soft bones clutched by sponges
And coral; tender muscles cupped
In razor shells; breasts, thighs stroked by
Kelp and foam; water touching her everywhere,
Coiling over her brightest flickerings,
Entering all her holes at once.

My landscape weeps and simpers,
Professing its history to Wanda,
But she is rubbed by the currents,
Sinks away into darkest water.

I sweat like a man who has swallowed
Too much salt. The pure god cannot
Understand my envy now, my heat
And confusion over this deepest void.

ZIMMER AND THE GHOST

We are like the masters of a lost dog,
Suddenly remembering all the sweet things
That she was. But the fine bitch has
Turned over. Wanda is dead and
None of us really knew who she was.

She was the best of us,
Always had courage to depart,
To frighten us by moving beyond bounds,
But now she has gone too far.
She will not come to us again.

Yesterday I thought I saw a ghost in
The strangled light of the ancient field.
" Z i m m e r ! " it lisped at me
As it fumed out of loose sod,
Its leering face a bag
Of working maggots and its hands
and nails clacking and constricting.
" Z i m m e r ! " it called.

I thought it was an elm stump beckoning,
A fencepost or a buckthorn blowing,
Even as I hoped that it was Wanda.
But as I walked toward it, my left eye
Twitched, my fingertips froze,
And my heart rammed the inside
Of my ribs.

It was nothing, of course;
And I had wanted it to be Wanda,
Had wanted to be baffled once again!

Wanda! When I am a ghostly spirit
Rising wormy and long-buried to walk
The earth again, I'll never toy with
My victims nor simply be a flicker
In the corner of their frightened eyes.
I will rise up in all my pearly,
Frozen essence, grinding my snags
And moaning like an albino walrus.
I will look my victim squarely under
Her sweating eyebrows, and ask,
"D o   y o u   l o v e   m e ? "
And if she answers yes, then—
And only then—will I fade.

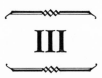

III

Cúchulainn said to Cethern:

"You had no right to kill those healers. We'll get no one to come to you now."

"They had no right to give me bad news."

The Tain
—*Translated by Thomas Kinsella*

THE GREAT HOUSE

Over and over it happens, my wife and I are
Out walking, we come to a great stone house
Built into a hillside. We are young again;
All things seem possible on this perfect day.
Suddenly we know that the house is ours!
We enter in joy, exulting in what we own:
Circular staircases, niches, ballrooms,
A dozen rooms full of leatherbound books,
Lace curtains, puppet theatres, daguerreotypes,
Chests full of doilies and ancient manuscript,
Hand printing presses, bowls of potpourri;
There are antique cribs, rocking chairs,
A canopied bed. We could start our lives again!
All windows swing open to singing birds and trees
Through which we see a whitewashed, sunlit city.

At night, after a lingering dinner and wine,
Lieder and string quartets by candle glow,
We ascend the tower, open the skylight
And turn the huge reflector into position.
The shimmer that we see has traveled for eons.
Under the circling stars, the birds against
The moon, with the vast rooms breathing
Beneath us, we know that the only sadness
In the world will be to leave this house.

for Suzanne

A FINAL AFFECTION

I love the accomplishments of trees,
How they try to restrain great storms
And pacify the very worms that eat them.
Even their deaths seem to be considered.

I fear for trees, loving them so much.
I am nervous about each scar on bark,
Each leaf that browns. I want to
Lie in their crotches and sigh,
Whisper of sun and rains to come.

Sometimes on summer evenings I step
Out of my house to look at trees
Propping darkness up to the silence.

When I die I want to slant up
Through those trunks so slowly
I will see each rib of bark, each whorl;
Up through the canopy, the subtle veins
And lobes touching me with final affection;
Then to hover above and look down
One last time on the rich upliftings,
The circle that loves the sun and moon,
To see at last what held the darkness up.

ZIMMER'S LOVE POEM
AFTER A HARD DREAM

I

In my most spectacular, technicolored dream
The great leaves slap my eyelids
As I smash through vegetation in pursuit
Of my rutting lady. My meat extends
And wavers like a pine log as I see
Her hard cheeks grinding through the bushes,
Her leg muscles bunching and breasts
Sliding like volcanos. Oh sun!
My lady could crush me if she got advantage,
But I stun her with a great stone
And she goes down on her back,
Roaring like a hairy brontosaurus.
Oh then it is I spread her,
And crushed between her incredible thighs,
As pterosaurs clack and duckbills belch,
I raise the human race within my loins
And fire it off to home!

II

All my dreams are for you,
All the glimmers of my organs
Burning into warm humus,
All the doorways like suddenly
Blossoming arbors that you
Appear in, the sun that
You leaf in, the paths down
Which you diminish in anger
And the rain in which you swell.

The wind full of risings
And fallings and darkness
Full of the memory of them,
These are for you.
I am the shrub that shelters
The neat rows of our garden,
You are the inside of my poems,
The light side of my leaves.
Together we graft our love
Quietly onto the world.

AN ENZYME POEM FOR SUZANNE

What a hulking bore it must be for you!
I slog along, ignoring you like my heart beat.
I gurgle and mold like an old fruit cellar,
Then suddenly you'll walk through a door
And foam me up like ancient cider in heat.
Then I'll fall all about you, blathering
With lost time, making you numb with words,
Wanting to mix our molecules, trying
To tell you of weeks in fifteen minutes.
Sometimes you must wonder what the hell
It is with Zimmer.
                    This is to tell you
That you are my enzymes, my yeast,
All the things that make my cork go pop.

ZIMMER LOATHING THE GENTRY

Their faces are like fine watches
Insinuating jewels.
Their movements can buy or sell you.
When the legs of the gentry dance for charity,
Meat splashes in the soups of the poor.
The eyes of the gentry are polished and blown,
When they look at you, you are worthless.
The gentry protect their names like hymens,
They suck their names like thumbs,
But they sign their names and something happens.
While, Zimmer, I can write, Zimmer,
All day, and nothing happens.

SONNET: ZIMMER IMAGINES HIMSELF BEING POET-IN-RESIDENCE

There is so much to look forward to:
I will reside in a house that is chanted,
In rooms that are quoted by echoes,
The faucets will run with metaphor,
And the toilets will flush down prose.
Beds will be for headlong dreaming,
All thermostats and meters start
The purest and most honest sentences.

I will not eat or drink in the residence.
My veins will flow with truth and art.
Outdoors sunlight will flash and bend enchanted,
Rain will break it down to purest glimmer.
Students will ask, "Who resides in that house?"
The wind and stars will answer, "Zimmer."

for Stan and Marie Felver

DRIVING NORTH FROM SAVANNAH
ON MY BIRTHDAY

Surely I pass most signs without seeing them,
Not the squares and octagons of the road,
But twirls of scud, magic rings of fungi,
Marks that tree limbs scribble
On the sky, subtle dances of insects,
Veering of flocks of birds,
Things that form and point to me,
Signs that might have shown me
How to live the rest of my life.

Forty-four years old today.
I think, too, of the minutes I have lived.
Twenty-two million yellow butterflies
Migrating south, sailing and turning,
Tying intricate love knots over the road.
I wipe them out by the thousands,
Driving my car hard north
Against their fragile yearnings.

ZIMMER FEARING ANEMIA

*Most country people around Transylvania look blank when asked if
they ever heard of the vampire Dracula.*—New York Times

Nobody sucks blood in Transylvania anymore.
The fusty castles have lost their shadows,
Being broken open to the sunlight.
Stakes are used exclusively as lot marks,
And pale ladies are presumed safe now
In their four-poster beds. The peasants
Believe that Bela Lugosi is a brand of goulash.
They laughed at the ancient legends.
But they don't feel as bad as I do,
They haven't seen or heard what I have;
How the elf owl peered through
Dry ice fog and screamed when
The kill was made, how gypsy bears
Moaned beneath the mike booms,
And the moon glared like the eye
Of a wolf through clouds that spun
Like flax within the filtered lenses.

Nobody believes that blood is sucked
In Transylvania anymore; but there are days
When I feel so bad, when my head seems
Like a prune and my body is folding, folding,
That I find myself fingering my neck
To be sure that two little holes aren't there.

for Fred Hetzel

WHEN ANGELS CAME TO ZIMMER

One morning a great gaggle slid
Down through holes in clouds,
Twirling like maple seeds
Through trees to the windowscreen.
Fervent as new tussock moths,
They flapped and dashed themselves,
Smearing their heavenly dust,
Until Zimmer, in pity and alarm,
Opened to let them into his study.
They flew in with smiles and sighs,
Making him bashful, as if a dozen
Gorgeous chorus girls had suddenly
Pranced into the room.
                    They perched on
Bookshelves, cigar stubs and beer cans;
One even tried to sit on Zimmer's lap.
All day they danced the Lindy,
And some, not knowing better, dabbled
Their darling toes in the toilet bowl.
They sang chorus after chorus of
"Stardust" and "Moonlight In Vermont,"
Constantly touching and stroking Zimmer.
Then at day's end, as if someone
Had rung a bell, they stood to sing
A final chorus of "Deep Purple."
With a whoosh of air and expensive perfume,
They fluttered from the room and ascended.
Zimmer stepped out to watch them rise
And flapped his dirty hankie at the stars.

Death of the Hired Zimmer

She sat watching the moth at the candle,
Waiting for Eli. When he came home
She ran to tell him. "Zimmer is back.
I saw him step out of the woods
At noon, look both ways, then head
For our place. What can we do?"

"Be calm," Eli said. "Was he alone?"

"Only his shadow, a bulge in his pocket.
Eli, be kind," she said and took
The market things from his arms.
"Don't laugh at him. He has a plan."
"I'll go and see him now," he said.
"You sit and watch the moon slide
Through that patch of clouds."
       He went,
Came back too soon, it seemed to her.
 "Dead?" she questioned
As he sat down.
  "Drunk," was all he answered.

WORK

To have done it thirty years
Without question! Yet I tell myself
I am grateful for all work;
At noon in my air-conditioned office
With a sandwich and a poem,
I try to recollect nature;
But a clerk comes in with papers
To be signed. I tell myself
The disruption does not matter;
It is all work: computer runs,
Contracts, invoices, poems; the same
As breaking shells, hunting woods,
Making pots or gathering grain.
Jazzmen even refer to sex as work.
Some primitive people believe
That death is work. When my wife asks
What I am doing, I always answer,
I am working, working, working.

Now I know I will spend the rest
Of my life trying for perfect work,
A work as rare as aurora borealis,
So fine it will make all other work
Seem true, that will last as long
As words will last. At home
In my room, I mumble to myself
Over my poems; over supper I talk
To myself; as I carpenter or paint
Or carry the groceries up the steps,
I am speaking words to myself.
"What are you doing?" my children ask.
I am working, working, working.

ZIMMER WARNS HIMSELF
WITH VIVID IMAGES AGAINST OLD AGE

Well, Zimmer, old reeking cricket,
There you go sliding your galoshes
Along cement as dismal and
Hard as your petrified bowels,
Your hands like frayed moths
Raising a yellow snot rag
To your swampy nostrils.
With your eyes unplugged now
Behind the fly-specked spectacles,
Your knees squawking, elbows flaring,
Joints burning, penis trickling,
Feet dead and teeth long gone,
You pay now with mumbling for
All the money you never saved
And all the poems you ever wrote.

ZIMMER FINDS IMBELLIS
IN THE ANCIENT GRAVES

I had not expected Imbellis here,
Gnarled like blackened dung beneath
The low tranquility of the bog,
In a mulch of shattered swords and caltrops,
Amidst fussing of morning birds,
Reeds moving in the wind of dragonflies
Squaring of the watery peat.
                    Imbellis, who was
Dealt out cell by cell to calcium and ancient gods
A thousand years ago, in his cape and bonnet,
Beside his broken halberd and shield cleaved
Down to its handle, he smells of moss on
Ancient stone, crumbles away like old halters.

How long can a nightmare last? I know it is
Always possible to be frightened by Imbellis.
I see his lips pulled back from his teeth,
Whiskers still fringed about his jagged scars,
Brow covered over his antique anger;
And though he is only cold stone,
I remember his havoc
And his energy,
Can feel it rising from
The clods again as though
He could uncoil like a spring
To knock men skittering into
A double vision of pain,
Unclench his teeth again
To say, "Zimmer," with derision.

As always I draw away
From him in a cold sweat,
My cheeks atwitch,
Balls clutching and rising,
I hold my arms high
To parry his blows.

DEATH DEMONSTRATES HIS PRESENCE
TO ZIMMER

I almost strangled on an almond,
Two weeks later I almost drowned.
Twice in a month death said,
"Hello, Zimmer," and showed me
Who is boss. I wanted to yank
His reserved seat out and send
Him clattering, but I was busy
Just trying to stay alive.

I swallowed the almond whole and crossways
And the river tried to swallow me.
By the time we had dislodged each other
My vision doubled and darkened,
And I was on my knees to
Old Mortality's parched phalanges.

When I was young I used to spit
In the insufferable eye of death,
Blow him apart with a loaded cigar
And offer him only the wormy apples.

But I had never almost died before.

Twice in a month death touched
My intolerant lungs, and now I feel him
On each frigid wind off the river
That blows the blossoms from the almond trees,
In every alien tingle of my fingertips and toes.

ZIMMER IMAGINES HEAVEN

I sit with Joseph Conrad in Monet's garden.
We are listening to Yeats chant his poems,
A breeze stirs through Thomas Hardy's moustache,
John Skelton has gone to the house for beer,
Wanda Landowska lightly fingers a clavichord,
Along the spruce tree walk Roberto Clemente and
Thurman Munson whistle a baseball back and forth.
Mozart chats with Ellington in the roses.

Monet smokes and dabs his canvas in the sun,
Brueghel and Turner set easels behind the wisteria.
The band is warming up in the Big Studio:
Bean, Brute, Bird and Serge on saxes,
Kai, Bill Harris, Lawrence Brown, trombones,
Little Jazz, Clifford, Fats on trumpets,
Klook plays drums, Mingus bass, Bud the piano.
Later Madam Schumann-Heink will sing Schubert,
The monks of Benedictine Abbey will chant.
There will be more poems from Emily Dickinson,
James Wright, John Clare, Walt Whitman.
Shakespeare rehearses players for *King Lear*.

At dusk Alice Toklas brings out platters
Of Sweetbreads à la Napolitaine, Salad Livonière,
And a tureen of Gaspacho of Malaga.
After the meal Brahms passes fine cigars.
God comes then, radiant with a bottle of cognac,
She pours generously into the snifters,
I tell Her I have begun to learn what
Heaven is about. She wants to hear.
It is, I say, being thankful for eternity.
Her smile is the best part of the day.

for Merrill Leffler

ZIMMER DIRECTS HIMSELF HOME
FROM THE DIGGINGS

Zimmer, you are getting sloppy;
You begin to worry about permanent damages:
The yellow and pink guts
Of the last sunfish from the pond,
Ripped out the same as a tree root.
You fuss about your hollow tooth,
Stinking pools in strip mines,
Small scatterings of bird bones,
Fine thoughts that you've never
Had time to think; you keep remembering
The same cruelties, distant pain,
All harming of the landscape.

It's time to go home, Zimmer,
You feel the future burning in
The dark folds of your stomach.
Your heart is tapping out despair.
You begin to feel sorry for yourself.

Move out with the sun, Zimmer!
You go straight on the old tracks,
Follow smoke through the mountain notch,
Go with ruts, stream and log,
Follow the shine of water home.
Avoid deer tracks and berry bushes
Because they lead you to bear.
If the sun sets and no moon rises,
Follow beacon fires under the swirl
Of stars, stay with the hollow road,
Go with tree clumps, sight to mounds.

It is a gentling process,
Turning into an animal.
There is hardly any pain.
Stones, grass, mushrooms, leaves,
All seem to flow up your legs
Into the movement of your blood.
Your nose becomes moist,
Fleas in your hair roots leap,
Tartar on your teeth turns green.
The earth becomes your only comfort.
You rest in a hollow tree
Or a place cleared in a bramble bush;
At last you are sleeping
Where you have always wanted to be.

PITT POETRY SERIES

Ed Ochester, General Editor

Dannie Abse, *Collected Poems*
Claribel Alegría, *Flowers from the Volcano*
Jack Anderson, *Toward the Liberation of the Left Hand*
Jon Anderson, *In Sepia*
Jon Anderson, *Looking for Jonathan*
John Balaban, *After Our War*
Michael Benedikt, *The Badminton at Great Barrington; Or, Gustave Mahler & the Chattanooga Choo-Choo*
Michael Burkard, *Ruby for Grief*
Kathy Callaway, *Heart of the Garfish*
Lorna Dee Cervantes, *Emplumada*
Robert Coles, *A Festering Sweetness: Poems of American People*
Leo Connellan, *First Selected Poems*
Fazıl Hüsnü Dağlarca, *Selected Poems*
Norman Dubie, *Alehouse Sonnets*
Stuart Dybek, *Brass Knuckles*
Odysseus Elytis, *The Axion Esti*
John Engels, *Blood Mountain*
John Engels, *Signals from the Safety Coffin*
Brendan Galvin, *The Minutes No One Owns*
Brendan Galvin, *No Time for Good Reasons*
Gary Gildner, *Digging for Indians*
Gary Gildner, *First Practice*
Gary Gildner, *Nails*
Gary Gildner, *The Runner*
Bruce Guernsey, *January Thaw*
Mark Halperin, *Backroads*
Patricia Hampl, *Woman Before an Aquarium*
Michael S. Harper, *Song: I Want a Witness*
John Hart, *The Climbers*
Samuel Hazo, *Blood Rights*
Samuel Hazo, *Once for the Last Bandit: New and Previous Poems*
Samuel Hazo, *Quartered*
Gwen Head, *Special Effects*
Gwen Head, *The Ten Thousandth Night*
Milne Holton and Graham W. Reid, eds., *Reading the Ashes: An Anthology of the Poetry of Modern Macedonia*
Milne Holton and Paul Vangelisti, eds., *The New Polish Poetry: A Bilingual Collection*
David Huddle, *Paper Boy*

Lawrence Joseph, *Shouting at No One*
Shirley Kaufman, *The Floor Keeps Turning*
Shirley Kaufman, *From One Life to Another*
Shirley Kaufman, *Gold Country*
Ted Kooser, *Sure Signs: New and Selected Poems*
Larry Levis, *Wrecking Crew*
Robert Louthan, *Living in Code*
Tom Lowenstein, tr., *Eskimo Poems from Canada and Greenland*
Archibald MacLeish, *The Great American Fourth of July Parade*
Peter Meinke, *Trying to Surprise God*
Judith Minty, *In the Presence of Mothers*
James Moore, *The New Body*
Carol Muske, *Camouflage*
Leonard Nathan, *Dear Blood*
Leonard Nathan, *Holding Patterns*
Kathleen Norris, *The Middle of the World*
Sharon Olds, *Satan Says*
Gregory Pape, *Border Crossings*
Thomas Rabbitt, *Exile*
James Reiss, *Express*
Ed Roberson, *Etai-Eken*
Eugene Ruggles, *The Lifeguard in the Snow*
Dennis Scott, *Uncle Time*
Herbert Scott, *Groceries*
Richard Shelton, *Of All the Dirty Words*
Richard Shelton, *Selected Poems, 1969-1981*
Richard Shelton, *You Can't Have Everything*
Gary Soto, *The Elements of San Joaquin*
Gary Soto, *The Tale of Sunlight*
Gary Soto, *Where Sparrows Work Hard*
David Steingass, *American Handbook*
Tomas Tranströmer, *Windows & Stones: Selected Poems*
Alberta T. Turner, *Lid and Spoon*
Chase Twichell, *Northern Spy*
Constance Urdang, *The Lone Woman and Others*
Constance Urdang, *Only the World*
Ronald Wallace, *Tunes for Bears to Dance To*
Cary Waterman, *The Salamander Migration and Other Poems*
Bruce Weigl, *A Romance*
David P. Young, *The Names of a Hare in English*
Paul Zimmer, *Family Reunion: Selected and New Poems*